DRESS SENSE

CLOTHES OF THE MEDIEVAL WORLD

CHRISTINE HATT

Illustrated by DANUTA MAYER

Belitha Press

First published in the UK in 2001 by

Belitha Press Limited, London House,

Great Eastern Wharf, Parkgate Road,

London SW11 4NQ

ISBN 1 84138 139 X

British Library Cataloguing in Publication Data
for this book is available from the British Library.

Series editor: Claire Edwards
Series designer: Angie Allison
Illustrator: Danuta Mayer
Picture researcher: Diana Morris
Consultant clothing historian: Dr Jane Bridgeman
Education consultant: Anne Washtell

Printed in Singapore

10 9 8 7 6 5 4 3 2 1

Picture acknowledgements:

Sonia Halliday Photographs: 7t.

Musée de la Tapisserie, Bayeux/Bridgeman
Art Library: 7b.

National Museum, Copenhagen: 6t.

V&A Museum/Bridgeman Art Library: 6b.

Page 23 bottom left: illustration based on the original illustration
by Angus McBride, from Men at Arms 259 The Mamluks
1250–1517 © Osprey Publishing Ltd.

**The cover picture shows a rich Italian couple of the
fifteenth century. The man is wearing brightly coloured
hose, a brocade doublet and tabard, and a balloon-
crowned hat. The woman is dressed in a tight-fitting
undergown, an overgown with hanging sleeves and a
pearl-decorated headdress.**

CONTENTS

Words in **bold** are explained in the glossary.

INTRODUCTION

This book will show you what people from many lands wore in medieval times. This period of history is known as the **Middle Ages**. It began in about 500 AD, after the fall of the Roman Empire. It then continued for about 1000 years until the **Byzantine Empire** had ended, Christopher Columbus had landed in the Americas and the **Renaissance** was well under way.

Continuity...

In the early Middle Ages, many people in the Byzantine Empire and Western Europe wore the same styles as they had worn in Roman times. The most common items of clothing were tunics of different lengths, designs and fabrics. Men sometimes wore trousers of various types, including short or long **breeches**, underneath them. These garments had all been introduced by invading peoples from Northern Europe and Asia.

...and change

Change gradually came, for several reasons. Contact with other peoples often led to new styles of dress. Rich Byzantines, for example, copied costume styles from nearby Persia. The different textiles available at different times also affected dress. For example, when wars blocked the **Silk Roads** from the seventh to the ninth centuries, few clothing silks reached the West. But then Italian merchants and others slowly began to import goods again. By the thirteenth century, a steady flow of fine fabrics was arriving in Europe. At the same time, Italy began to develop its own silk-making industry.

This seventh-century Frank (see pages 10–11) is dressed in garments of early medieval Europe. He wears **braies** tucked into short **hose**, under a tunic with embroidered edges. Linen strips hold the hose in place.

Here, a prince is dressed in rich clothes of late medieval Europe. Under his cloak he wears a short **doublet** with a jewelled belt around the hips. His legs are covered in close-fitting hose.

Rich women in fourteenth-century Europe often wore **surcoats** with cut-away sides that showed close-fitting gowns underneath. The cloak and **caul** are also typical of the period.

Fitting fashion

The monarchs of thirteenth-century Western Europe ruled **feudal** societies in which the population and trade were increasing. Kings, queens and nobles used rich fabrics, as well as furs from Northern Europe, to make beautiful costumes. By this time, clothes-makers were starting to **tailor** garments to fit wearers more tightly. This may have been because, as people grew richer, they could afford to throw away the scraps of fabric wasted when cloth is cut to fit. Since the Middle Ages, Europeans have always worn tailored clothes.

About this book

The next two pages show you how experts know what medieval people wore. Each double page that follows describes the clothing of a particular place and time. Material Matters boxes give more information on types of material from which clothes were made. Other boxes give information on special subjects such as hairstyles or jewellery. There is a brief timeline at the top of each page, and maps on pages 44–45 help you find some of the places mentioned in this book.

What is a costume?

A garment is an individual item of clothing. A costume is a set of clothes designed to be worn together.

From the seventh century, **Muslim Arabs conquered many lands. People in areas of the world that they invaded, such as North Africa, copied their loose robes and other garments. The Arab on the camel below wears a thirteenth-century robe made of rich cloth.**

Around the World

Travel, trade and religious warfare brought new clothes to the medieval inhabitants of Western Europe, but people in other parts of the world continued to dress in traditional garments. In China the long *p'ao robes* of ancient times were still worn. In South and Central America, Incas and Aztecs continued to wear woven tunics and cloaks. In Africa, loincloths and draped robes remained common. Costume in many of these areas did not change greatly until after the fifteenth century, when the West began to spread its culture around the globe through conquest and trade.

HOW WE KNOW

Costume experts use a wide range of evidence to work out what people wore in the **Middle Ages**. They examine the garments and fragments of cloth that have survived. They look at medieval paintings, statues and other forms of art. Finally, they look at descriptions of clothing found in books and documents of the time.

Rare survivals

Complete or nearly complete garments give the most accurate information, but only a few have survived. One example is a silk cloak that was made for King Roger II of Sicily in 1133 (see page 19). The date the garment was made was woven into the fabric. A fourteenth-century robe that belonged to Queen Margaret of Denmark still exists too (see right).

Garments from the grave

Most medieval Christians were buried unclothed in linen shrouds, but kings, queens and nobles were often dressed in fine clothes. These garments usually fell to pieces in the grave, but experts can use cloth scraps to build up a picture of the original outfits. For example, fabric found in the tomb of a sixth-century Merovingian queen (see page 10) showed that she wore a linen **chemise** with a violet silk robe and red silk tunic.

Information from art

Works of art in medieval churches, such as sculptures, mosaics, **frescoes** and stained glass windows, show people and their clothing in great detail. Medieval Bibles and other books were often illustrated with paintings of people in scenes from everyday life. Tapestries are another useful source of clothing information.

Books of hours were used by ordinary people to tell them all the prayers that they should say at fixed times of the day. They were often illustrated with pictures of people wearing the costumes of the time. This painting is from a book of hours that was made in France in about 1416, for the Duc de Berry.

This gown is more than 600 years old and belonged to Queen Margaret of Denmark, Sweden and Norway. It is made of red and gold brocade, and has a tight bodice and a long, full skirt.

The 70.5m-long Bayeux Tapestry is really an embroidery. It was made in eleventh-century England and shows the conquest of England by the **Normans** in 1066. English and Norman clothing appears in colourful detail. The tapestry is kept in a museum in Bayeux, France.

Handle with care

Experts have to take care when they study works of art to find out what people wore. A painting made at a certain time may not show people dressed in the clothes of that time. For example, medieval religious art showed some Bible characters dressed in late Roman styles of clothing. It is also hard to judge fabric colours from paintings. Many have faded, and early medieval artists could not always make paint that matched clothing dyes.

By the book

Few medieval books were written especially to describe costume. One that has survived is the *Book of Ceremonies*, which contains exact rules about what everyone at the Byzantine court (see pages 8–9) should wear. Luckily, medieval histories and stories give more information about clothing. Experts can also study documents such as wills in which people listed the garments that they were leaving to family members.

A twelfth-century carving from the outside of Chartres Cathedral in France. It shows shepherds dressed in the clothes of medieval peasants. They are wearing short tunics, rough **breeches**, and a cloak or hooded cape.

Popes and Peasants

Medieval art shows the costumes of popes, kings and other powerful people far more often than those of poor peasants. Rich people's clothes have also survived more often than those of the poor. As a result, more is known about the luxury garments of the Middle Ages than about any other kind of medieval clothing.

330
Emperor Constantine founds a
second capital in Byzantium.

391
Christianity made the state religion
in Rome. Pagan religions banned.

410
Rome sacked by
invading Visigoths.

476
Last Roman emperor deposed
by Goths. End of the Roman Empire.

THE BYZANTINE EMPIRE

A famous mosaic in Italy
shows this Byzantine
empress wearing a
jewelled diadem and
Persian-style collar.

This seventh-century
earring is made of
gold, sapphires,
emeralds and pearls.

The Byzantines were
Christians and many
wore crosses. This cross
is made from gold and
enamel.

In 330 AD, the Roman emperor Constantine founded a second capital in the city of Byzantium. He renamed the city Constantinople and ruled from there and Rome. After Rome was invaded, Constantinople was the only capital. The area it ruled became known as the **Byzantine Empire**. This empire included parts of Asia and Europe, so clothing was influenced by fashions from both.

Eastern influences

At first, wealthy people in the Byzantine Empire wore tunics and simple, draped garments in Roman styles. Then, gradually, Eastern-style decorations such as tassels, embroidery and jewels were added. Fabrics became richer and more colourful, too. New garments were also introduced from the East. For example, the Persian **caftan** was worn at the Byzantine court from the twelfth century.

Imperial splendour

Early emperors and empresses often wore just a silk tunic with a cloak on top. Later, other items, such as the *loros* (a kind of wrap), were worn over the tunic. New forms of dress also developed. The last Byzantine emperors often wore a caftan or a *saccos*, a type of stiff, full-length robe (see right). Fabrics became heavier and stiffer as they were decorated with more gold embroidery and jewels.

Tunics and trousers

The Byzantine poor usually wore short tunics and Persian-style leggings that could be close-fitting or loose. Sometimes the tunics were pulled up at the sides to make it easier to walk. Rich men and women wore leggings, too. They were often decorated with bands of embroidery. Some had jewels sewn down the back.

Byzantine men often wore
caps like this one, called a
Phrygian cap. The point
flopped over to the front
because the cap was made
of soft material.

A workman dressed in
close-fitting, Persian-style
leggings. The legs are
separate and tied to a belt
under the tunic. The man
has pulled up his tunic so
that he can move freely.

CHANGING STYLES
SIXTH AND ELEVENTH CENTURY

The picture on the left shows the Byzantine emperor Justinian, who ruled from 527 to 565. He is wearing a white silk tunic embroidered with gold. It ends below the knee, but emperors often wore full-length tunics and empresses always did. His cloak is purple silk, which only the royal family could wear. It is fastened with a jewelled clasp. The gold panel on the cloak is called a tablion, and is a sign of rank. Justinian's **diadem** headdress has pearls hanging from the sides.

The picture on the right shows the eleventh-century Byzantine emperor Romanus IV. He has a *loros* draped around his tunic and up over his right arm. It is embroidered with gold and covered with jewels.

Religious Robes

Russia had strong trading links with Constantinople, and ideas as well as goods passed along the trade routes. In the tenth century, the Russians adopted the **Orthodox Christianity** of the Byzantine Empire. Today, the priests of the Greek and Russian Orthodox Church still wear garments like those worn by this late Byzantine emperor (see right). Among them are a bishop's robe and mitre (hat) similar to the *saccos* robe and closed crown shown here.

MATERIAL MATTERS

Byzantine rulers always wore silks, which were famous for their beauty. By the sixth century, all stages of the Byzantine silk industry were well established. They included the cultivation of silkworms, the dyeing of silk thread and the weaving of silk cloth. Popular cloth designs later included circles and mythical beasts, as well as eagles and rosettes (above). The silks were made in workshops attached to the imperial palace in Constantinople and elsewhere in the empire.

THE FRANKS

The Franks were a group of **Germanic** peoples who conquered part of the Roman Empire in the fourth century AD. They established a kingdom that spread across the area of Western Europe where France and Germany now lie.

Collecting the evidence

The first **dynasty** to rule the Frankish Kingdom was the Merovingian, set up by Clovis in 481. Merovingians were buried in their clothes, so experts have learned about their costume from fabric and jewellery found in graves (see page 6). Illustrated Bibles and church carvings of the era also give information about what people wore.

Embroidered tunics

Merovingian men usually dressed in knee-length, sleeved tunics. These garments often had embroidered bands around the hem and cuffs. They were usually made from linen and wool, but metal-plated leather tunics were worn for fighting. Men wore knee-length or full-length *braies* under their tunics, sometimes with short **hose** (see page 4). They wound linen strips over the *braies* or hose from below the knee on to the feet. Experts know less about women's clothing, but believe that most women wore one or two long tunics. They were often decorated with embroidered bands around the neck and cuffs.

Carolingian clothing

In 752, the Merovingian dynasty was replaced by the Carolingian dynasty. Its greatest king was Charlemagne (see right), who ruled the Frankish Kingdom from 768 to 814. Clothing changed little during this time, but new fashions included boots with laces for men and hair nets decorated with jewels for women.

This gold statue, which dates from about the fifth century AD, was discovered in France. It shows a man wearing a short tunic covered in square, possibly metal, ornaments.

The Frankish helmet above is made from two pieces of bronze that have been joined at the top by heating the metal. It may have had a crest attached to the ridge.

Frankish women who wore only one tunic often draped a wrap on top. It was pulled up over the head and fastened with a brooch on the shoulder.

MATERIAL MATTERS

Fine silks for clothing were imported into the Frankish Kingdom from the **Byzantine Empire**. But Merovingians made their own woollen fabrics, working patterns such as spots, flowers and trefoils (shapes like clover leaves) into the weave.

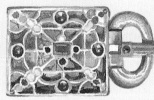

Frankish Jewellery

The Franks wore a wide range of jewellery, including **fibulae** brooches (left), which were used to hold cloaks and tunics in place, necklaces, earrings and even belt buckles (below left). These ornaments were often made of gold or silver, and set with **enamels**, stones such as amber, or pearls. Their styles were often based on imported Scandinavian designs.

CHARLEMAGNE'S COSTUMES NINTH CENTURY

In 800, the Frankish ruler Charlemagne became emperor of the **Western Christian Empire**. The picture on the left shows the Byzantine-style robes he wore for his coronation. He is dressed in a long white tunic with gold edging, and over this has a red, embroidered *dalmatica*. On top he has several **brocade** cloaks, including one made of square-patterned gold cloth, and another made of purple cloth. His red leather shoes have emeralds on them, and his gold crown is set with gems.

Emperor Charlemagne's everyday clothing, shown on the right, was simpler. He has a short tunic edged with coloured silk, and over this he wears a fur-lined cloak fastened with a brooch at the shoulder. His long linen *braies* are held in place with thin strips of leather attached to his shoes.

THE ANGLO-SAXONS

The Anglo-Saxons were a group of **Germanic** peoples who conquered much of England after the Romans left in 410 AD. By the seventh century, they had divided the land into seven warring kingdoms. Costume changed very little in Anglo-Saxon times, which ended in 1066. During this time, people wore a small range of simple styles.

Lots of layers

Anglo-Saxon women dressed in several layers of clothing. First they wore a full-length garment with tight-wristed sleeves called a smock. On top came a second, similar garment called a kirtle. Above these, women wore a looser **super-tunic** that had full sleeves ending below the elbow. It was sometimes pulled in with a waist belt on which purses and keys were hung for safekeeping.

Kings and commoners

Ordinary Anglo-Saxon men and the kings who ruled over them wore similar clothes – only the quality of the fabrics was different. Most men wore short tunics, sometimes with loose shirts on top, and short **breeches**. Poor people's clothes were often brown or grey, which are the natural colours of the wool from which they were made. Kings could afford clothes dyed bright colours such as red, and embroidered with gold.

Heads and feet

Anglo-Saxon women always covered their heads with a coverchief (veil). The fabric was left to hang loose around the face, or was wrapped around the neck or fastened with a brooch. Men sometimes wore skullcaps, which fitted the head closely, or Phrygian caps (see page 8). Both sexes wore leather shoes, often with pointed toes.

This woman is wearing a tight-sleeved smock (hidden) and green kirtle under a loose-sleeved super-tunic. She is holding a coverchief, which she would have worn in public.

Women wore cloaks over their clothes. The cloaks were draped so that they were longer at the back than the front.

Anglo-Saxon men often wore plain leather skullcaps.

This tenth-century Anglo-Saxon maniple (see box) was found in the tomb of St Cuthbert in Durham Cathedral. It is made of silk embroidered with silk and gold threads.

A KING AND A PRIEST   TENTH CENTURY

The man shown on the left is Athelstan, who ruled two separate Anglo-Saxon kingdoms before becoming King of all the English in 926 AD. This image is based on an Anglo-Saxon picture. It shows him wearing a white tunic edged with gold, red **hose** and a blue cloak. The bright colours were produced using vegetable dyes. The king wears an open crown made of gold on his head.

In the sixth century, Christianity was brought to the Anglo-Saxons from Ireland and Rome, then gradually spread. The Christian priest on the right is wearing a long **alb** under a finely embroidered **chasuble** cloak. He has a narrow scarf called a **maniple** over his arm.

Anglo-Saxon Jewellery

The Anglo-Saxons loved to wear jewellery. One of the most famous pieces of Anglo-Saxon jewellery is the Alfred Jewel (right, above). It is made of gold, rock crystal and **enamel** and shows the ninth-century king Alfred the Great. It was probably not made to be worn, but to fix on a pointer used to follow lines of text on a page. The silver Fuller Brooch (right), decorated with symbols of the five senses, was worn as an ornament.

MATERIAL MATTERS

In most Anglo-Saxon homes, women spun and wove sheep's wool to make fabric. Rich women also liked to spend their leisure hours creating beautiful embroideries to decorate clothing. They often used silk threads to make patterns and sometimes added jewels to the finished garments.

THE VIKINGS

The Vikings originally came from Norway, Sweden and Denmark. From the eighth century AD they began to raid and later to settle in many countries, including Britain, France, Russia, Greenland and, briefly, North America. Most Viking clothes were made of wool or linen, but the style and fabric varied according to the class of the wearer.

Archaeologists found these glass beads in York. Viking craftsmen often made beads by heating existing pieces of glass and forming them into shape around iron rods.

Men and women wore shoes that were usually made of cow leather. Many were slip-ons, but some had buckles, as shown here. Men also wore lace-up boots.

Buried treasure

Many Viking sites have provided useful information about costume and jewellery. Archaeologists discovered some of the best Viking garments at Hedeby, a harbour once in Denmark, but now part of Germany. Other important finds were made in the English city of York (Viking Jorvik). They included cloth scraps, leather shoes and glass beads.

Rich man, poor man

Wealthy Viking men often wore baggy trousers that were bound tightly to the lower leg with long cloth strips. Above this they wore a loose overshirt belted at the waist. The most usual form of outer garment was a short cloak fastened at the shoulder with a brooch, but jackets were also worn. The most common fabric was fine wool, sometimes dyed. Poor men also wore baggy trousers, bound or unbound, with a long-sleeved tunic. The rough wool of these garments was undyed.

This woman wears a calf-length pinafore dress over a full-length, long-sleeved tunic. Her hair is bound in a plait. Vikings often used combs made of deer antler to style their hair.

Viking women

Viking women wore a full-length, long-sleeved tunic made of linen or wool, with a shorter woollen pinafore dress on the top. The shoulder straps of the pinafore were fastened at the front with two brooches, and a third brooch was sometimes worn at the neck of the tunic. The finest brooches were made of gold and decorated with patterns.

This ornate gold pendant was discovered in the former Viking town of Hedeby (see main text).

MATERIAL MATTERS

The Vikings trapped many animals such as mink, **sable**, **ermine**, bear and otter for their furs. They used some for their own clothing, but traded the rest abroad. There they were often made into luxury coats for monarchs and nobles. Another important material traded by the Vikings was the orange-brown, semi-precious stone amber. This was often washed up along the shores of the Baltic Sea. It was made into jewellery.

A Viking Abroad

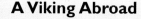

King Cnut of Denmark also ruled much of England from 1016 to 1035. This image comes from a picture that shows Cnut in Winchester. He is wearing garments with special features. Among them are his short **hose** with decorative embroidered tops and his cloak, which has a ring on its top edge. Experts believe that the cloak was fastened around the neck by pulling its ends through the ring.

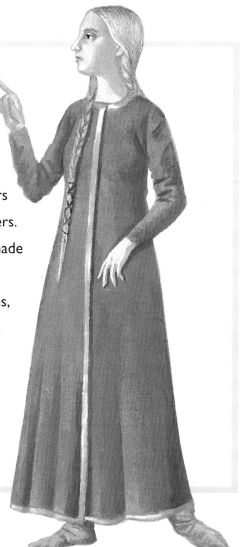

OUT AND ABOUT TENTH CENTURY

This wealthy Viking couple are dressed to go out in the cold of a Scandinavian winter. The man wears a shirt, which is laced at the neck, and blue trousers. His jacket is fitted and belted at the waist. It is made of thick wool and trimmed with a wide band of fur. The woman's garment, worn over her dresses, is also of wool and edged with gold tape. Experts believe that fitted coats of this type may have been quilted for extra warmth. Both the man and the woman are wearing short leather boots made of goatskin, which was more expensive than the usual cowhide.

VIKING WARRIORS

Viking warriors struck fear into the hearts of their enemies. Some wore metal body armour and helmets to protect themselves from blows. All carried deadly battle weapons such as swords, spears and axes.

Dressed for battle

Vikings who went on raids abroad did not dress in military uniforms. Kings and nobles, as well as soldiers who fought in private armies at home, usually wore armour. It was made up of two main garments – a leather tunic with a **chain mail** coat of metal rings over the top. Important men also wore iron helmets. Ordinary farmers who joined raids usually wore their everyday clothes.

Viking swords

The weapons that warriors used also depended on their status. The rich had finely crafted swords with double-edged blades. They were made of iron with razor-sharp steel on the cutting edges. Vikings also used short, single-edged knives called *screamasax*. Both swords and knives were carried in wood and leather covers called scabbards. These were often lined with fleeces to prevent the blades from rusting, and were sometimes decorated with bronze.

Spears and axes

Many fighting Vikings could not afford swords. Instead they used iron spears. There were two main types – one for thrusting into nearby enemies and one for throwing at enemies some distance away. Battle axes were also common – their triangular iron heads were known as bearded blades. Some Viking warriors were expert archers. They fired iron-tipped arrows from flexible bows made of yew and other woods.

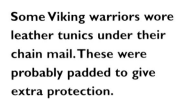

Some Viking warriors wore leather tunics under their chain mail. These were probably padded to give extra protection.

This tenth-century cross from Yorkshire shows a Viking warrior with his spear (left), shield (top right), sword (centre right) and axe (bottom right). On his belt is a scabbard for a *screamasax*.

The most costly Viking swords had decorated hilts (tops). Many also had grooves down the middle. These made the swords lighter to carry without reducing their cutting power.

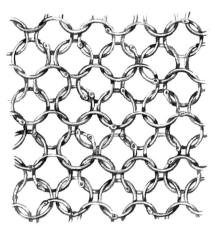

A close-up view of chain mail, showing the interlocking rings. Mail coats were often handed from father to son for several generations.

WARRIOR WEAR NINTH CENTURY

These two Vikings are ready for battle. The man on the left is a nobleman. He is wearing two layers of armour – a padded leather tunic under a chain mail coat belted at the waist. His domed iron helmet has a nose and eye guard at the front and a flap of chain mail at the back to protect his neck. His wooden shield is painted. It is also strengthened with an iron rim and has an iron boss (knob) in the centre. This is designed to stop stabs from enemy swords reaching his hand and making him drop the shield.

The man on the right is a Danish farmer who has gone a-viking (that is, joined a raiding expedition) with professional warriors. He wears his everyday woollen trousers and tunic, but also carries a wooden shield and a 'bearded blade' battle axe.

Sutton Hoo

In 1939, archaeologists unearthed a ship in Sutton Hoo, Suffolk. It was the burial site of a seventh-century Anglo-Saxon king (see page 12). The archaeologists discovered many fine treasures. They included an iron helmet decorated with bronze, silver and gold (above). It was probably made in Sweden and shows that Scandinavian craftsmen were making and trading high-quality objects long before they began their raids.

MATERIAL MATTERS

In many Scandinavian lakes, chemical reactions sometimes take place that make tiny particles of iron in the water form lumps of iron ore. This is called bog-iron. The Vikings collected it, **smelted** it, then used it to make their weapons. Viking blacksmiths were highly skilled. Using a technique called pattern-welding (see left), they combined irons of different types and strengths to make top-class fighting tools. Some Viking swords were also imported from the Frankish Kingdom (see page 10), where many other expert metal-workers lived.

EUROPE IN THE ELEVENTH AND TWELFTH CENTURIES

A twelfth-century Norman. Rich French- and Englishmen often wore long undertunics with shorter super-tunics on top. The super-tunics usually had patterned borders and flared sleeves.

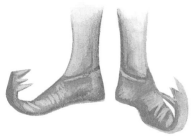

'Scorpion tail' shoes became popular in early twelfth-century France, and later in England too.

In about 1000 AD, many people in Western Europe were still wearing tunics and **breeches**. These had been popular for hundreds of years. But then, gradually, clothing styles began to change.

New styles

In France and many other European countries, two new garments were introduced, mainly among the rich. The first was a plain undertunic with long, tight sleeves. It was full-length for women, and usually a little shorter for men. On top of this, people wore a **super-tunic**. It was often belted, with decorative borders around the wrists and hem. Women's super-tunics became more close-fitting, apart from the sleeves, which were made loose and flared.

Breeches and hose

Men continued to wear breeches under their tunics. On their legs they usually wore stockings, called **hose**. These were made of wool, sometimes dyed bright colours, or linen. In the eleventh century, the hose usually covered only the lower leg, but by the twelfth century reached half way up the thigh. They were held up by strings attached to a belt round the waist. As hose became longer, breeches grew shorter, and were often tucked into the hose tops. Some men bound hose on with linen strips (see page 4).

Plaits and beards

Women continued to cover their hair with cloaks or veils. In the twelfth century, veils became lighter and the hair could be seen below them. It was often worn in two plaits bound with silk ribbons. Hair extensions were used to increase the length. Some eleventh-century men cut their hair short, but during the twelfth century long hair, as well as beards and moustaches, became more common.

People wore different types of belt round their super-tunics. The man's belt (top) has a buckle. The woman's belt (above) is fastened with knotted silk and bead cords.

In the twelfth century, super-tunic **bodices** were often laced at the back or sides. Here the bodice is laced so that you can see the undertunic beneath.

MATERIAL MATTERS

In the ninth century, Muslim Arabs conquered the Mediterranean island of Sicily. There they set up textile workshops that wove light silks decorated with animals, birds and flowers. Other silks were embroidered with richly coloured threads. The Sicilians continued to make these Eastern-style fabrics after their island was conquered by Normans (see right) in the eleventh century. Many were sold to **Crusaders** (see page 20) as they made their way to and from the Holy Land. This beautiful silk cloak was made in 1133 for Roger II, King of Sicily.

Tapestry Tales

The Vikings who settled in north-west France during the early tenth century became known as **Normans**. In 1066 the Normans invaded England – an event shown on the Bayeux Tapestry (see page 7). The tapestry tells us about Norman clothing of the eleventh century. It shows that many Norman men wore short tunics and had short hair, shaped into the neck at the back. The hair was then brushed forward to create a short fringe.

WOMEN'S WEAR
ELEVENTH AND TWELFTH CENTURIES

The Norman woman on the left is dressed in late eleventh-century style. She is wearing an embroidered **super-tunic** over a plain undertunic (hidden). Her super-tunic is pulled up slightly over the tasselled **braid** waist belt. Her **mantle** is draped loosely around her shoulders and fastened by a cord that links two clasps. The woman's veil covers her hair and neck.

The French noblewoman on the right is dressed in the style of the mid-twelfth century. She has a closer-fitting, lined super-tunic, belted at the waist with a jewelled double girdle (belt). The tunic sleeves flare out from the elbows. A fine, loose veil topped with a coronet covers the woman's hair. The ends of her long plaits are held in cylinders made of decorated metal.

KNIGHTS IN ARMOUR

From about 900, a new type of **cavalry** soldier emerged in Europe – the knight. At first knights served in the armies of kings and nobles. But from the late eleventh century, many took part in the **Crusades** as religious warriors. The era of the knight lasted until about 1500, and armour developed throughout this time.

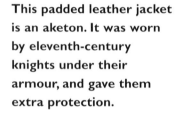

This padded leather jacket is an aketon. It was worn by eleventh-century knights under their armour, and gave them extra protection.

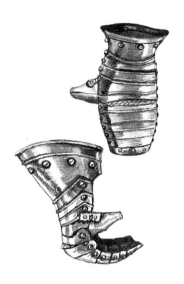

Plate armour gauntlets protected knights' hands and wrists. They were hinged to allow some movement, and were lined with leather.

Protective layers

In the eleventh century, knights wore three main layers over their ordinary clothes. First came the aketon, a padded jacket sometimes made of leather (see left). Over this was the hauberk, a tunic usually made of **chain mail**. The top layer of clothing was a light fabric **surcoat**. It was designed to reflect the sun's heat away from the knight inside his heavy metal armour.

Armour plating

Chain mail was uncomfortable. Worse still, swords could cut through it. So from the thirteenth century, knights began to wear plate armour made of sheet steel. At first, it was used to cover only parts of the body. Chain mail was still worn at the same time. In the fifteenth century, knights began to wear full suits of plate armour, weighing up to 25 kilograms.

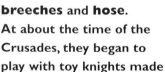

Norman boys usually wore short tunics, **breeches** and **hose**. At about the time of the Crusades, they began to play with toy knights made of wood and dressed in the armour of the period.

Knights often took part in tournaments, where they jousted. At first, they wore ordinary armour. But by the fifteenth century, jousting armour was more colourful than anything seen on the battlefield.

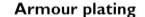

Helmet styles

The earliest types of helmet, worn with chain mail suits, were very simple. They had holes for the eyes and sometimes a crest on top decorated with the wearer's **coat of arms**. Helmets worn with plate armour had more features. For example, they had **visors** that could be raised and lowered.

BATTLE DRESS THIRTEENTH AND FIFTEENTH CENTURIES

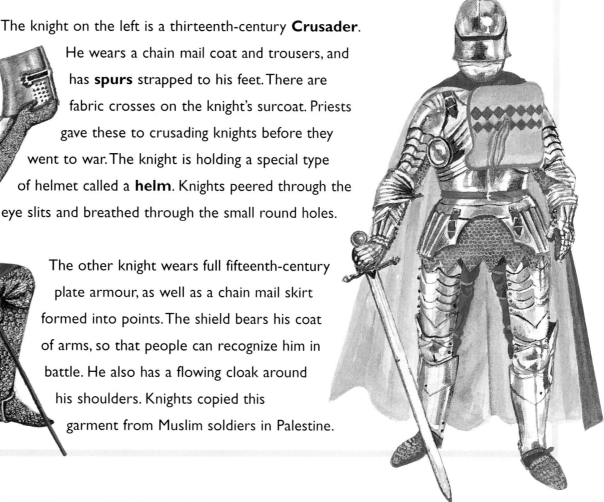

The knight on the left is a thirteenth-century **Crusader**. He wears a chain mail coat and trousers, and has **spurs** strapped to his feet. There are fabric crosses on the knight's surcoat. Priests gave these to crusading knights before they went to war. The knight is holding a special type of helmet called a **helm**. Knights peered through the eye slits and breathed through the small round holes.

The other knight wears full fifteenth-century plate armour, as well as a chain mail skirt formed into points. The shield bears his coat of arms, so that people can recognize him in battle. He also has a flowing cloak around his shoulders. Knights copied this garment from Muslim soldiers in Palestine.

Warrior Monks

From 1095 to 1270, Christian knights fought a series of wars known as the Crusades in Palestine. Their main aim was to seize the Holy Land from Muslims. Two military orders of monks, the Knights Hospitaller and Knights Templar, were set up to help ordinary knights in their campaigns. In battle, the Knights Templar wore white surcoats marked with a red cross, while the Knights Hospitaller wore red surcoats marked with a white cross.

MATERIAL MATTERS

Armour improved over the centuries not only because styles changed but because people learned how to make better-quality steel. The strong steel available by the fifteenth century was used to make the most protective armour ever. It was known as white armour because it was highly polished and not blackened to prevent rusting like other types of armour.

THE ISLAMIC WORLD

Islam was founded in early seventh-century Arabia by the Prophet Muhammad. By 750, the Arabs had carried their new faith as far as Spain in the west and Central Asia in the east. Two main costume styles were worn in this vast region – long, loose robes in Arabia, North Africa and the Mediterranean, and more fitted garments in Asia.

This linen tunic was made for a child in Egypt during the eleventh or twelfth century. The weaving and brown wool embroidery were influenced by local Christian styles.

Archaeologists discovered this fur-lined silk caftan in a Muslim prince's tomb in Central Asia. It was probably made during the eighth or ninth century.

Arab style

The Arabs dressed in simple clothes that protected them from the heat and dust of the day and the cool of the night. Most people wore ankle-length robes with long, wide sleeves. Cloaks were wrapped on top for warmth. Women often pulled their cloaks over their hair and some wore face veils too. Men wore turbans on their heads.

Give and take

As the Arabs travelled around the world, they copied clothes worn by peoples that they had conquered. They were also happy to learn new clothes-making techniques. For example, after the Arabs conquered Egypt, Muslim weavers were influenced by the textiles and garments made by the Christians there.

Asian style

The Arabs copied many clothing styles from the Persians, including the coatlike **caftan**. The caftan, like many clothes worn in Persia and Central Asia, was **tailored** to fit the body. The Arabs, and other Muslim peoples such as the Turks, also wore loose trousers pulled tight at the waist and ankles. This style probably came from the Persians too. Men usually wore the trousers under long tunics. Women often wore them with knee-length, belted robes.

This medieval Arab woman wears a short robe, belted at the waist, above baggy trousers. A shawl wound around her hair forms a headdress.

A decorated silk hat from medieval Egypt. A turban was probably wound around the edge so that only the top showed.

632–634	636–638	640–650	711	1095–1270	1492
Abu Bakr, Muhammad's father-in-law, unites the Arabs.	Arabs invade much of the Middle East.	Arabs invade North Africa and Persia.	Moors invade Spain and Portugal.	The Crusades.	Moors expelled from Spain by Christian troops.

MATERIAL MATTERS

Some of the most luxurious cloths in the medieval world were made in the Middle East. Many bundles were carried back to the West by knights and pilgrims. The English names of different types of cloth still show their origins. Patterned **damasks** came from Damascus in Syria and cotton **muslin** from Mosul in Iraq. A rich gold and silver **brocade** called baldachin came from Baghdad, now the capital city of Iraq.

Tiraz

During the **Middle Ages**, the garments of many Muslims were decorated with *tiraz*. These were bands made in weaving factories owned by the ruler of the time. They carried his name, the name of the factory and the date of production, as well as an Islamic inscription. Most were sewn on to clothes that the ruler gave to his servants and officials. The word '*tiraz*' comes from the Persian for embroidery, but the bands could also be woven or painted.

A TURK AND AN ARAB TWELFTH AND THIRTEENTH CENTURIES

The man on the left is a Mamluk, one of a class of Turkish warriors who fought in the **Crusades** and ruled Egypt from 1250 to 1517. He wears trousers and a **chain mail** hauberk (see page 20) under a woollen coat. The silver coins on his belt show that he is an officer. His special hat is called a *kalawta*.

The Arab man shown relaxing on the right is wearing a long, loose robe. It has decorated *tiraz* bands (see above) around the sleeves at the top and has been dyed bright red. This colour was usually produced using insect dyes such as **kermes**. On his head, the man wears a turban, sometimes known as the Crown of the Arabs. One end of the turban fabric trails loose at the back – this was a popular style.

23

EUROPE IN THE THIRTEENTH CENTURY

A German woman of the late thirteenth century. She is wearing a sleeveless overdress and has loose, uncovered hair. These show that she is not married.

During the thirteenth century, international trade in cloth and other goods grew, as new routes continued to open up between East and West. Cloth-making industries also developed in Europe, leading to the growth of a middle class of rich merchants. Like monarchs and nobles, they loved to show their status by wearing fine clothes.

New styles

For much of this century, rich men and women still dressed in tunics and **super-tunics**, but they wore various new items of clothing over them, such as the **surcoat**. This had developed from a garment worn by knights (see page 20). At first surcoats were calf-length and sleeveless, but later styles were made with sleeves. In Germany women wore overdresses. Unmarried girls wore a sleeveless overdress (see left), while older and married women wore a short-sleeved version.

Work wear

The poor still wore simple clothes of rough wool or **hemp**. Men dressed in short tunics or loose shirts, *braies* and **hose**. Women wore long, loose gowns over smocks. Both men and women had short, hooded capes. From about the twelfth century, side slits were added to tunics and *braies*. The slits made it easier for people to move while working and to tie clothing up out of the way.

Hats and headcoverings

Europeans covered their heads and necks with a variety of garments in this era. The wimple was popular among women (see left). Barbettes, fillets and crespines (see box, right) were also common. Many men wore a close-fitting cap, often with a chin-strap, called a coif.

The wimple was a rectangle of fabric pinned under the neck and on to the hair at each side. A loose veil was usually draped over the hair, too.

This style of hooded cloak was popular for men in the thirteenth century. They put their arms through holes in the cloak, and let the sleeves hang loose.

Nobles of this period often wore soft gloves made of calfskin or kidskin. They were probably decorated with huge jewels, such as rubies or even diamonds.

RICH AND POOR   THIRTEENTH CENTURY

The rich woman on the left is wearing a full tunic with a surcoat and cloak on top. The armholes of the surcoat are large, showing much of the garment underneath. The woman's hair is pulled into a type of bun called a chignon at the back, and is covered with a crespine (net). The barbette (band of white linen) under her chin is attached to a fillet (band of stiffened material) on her head.

The peasants on the right are dressed for harvesting. All have coifs on their heads. One man wears short linen *braies* with side slits (centre), while another has pulled his long *braies* up with cords (bottom). A third has tied his tunic up at the sides, showing hose laced to short *braies* underneath.

Trade Fairs

In the thirteenth century, textiles, furs and jewellery from abroad, as well as fine fabrics made in Europe, were sold at bustling trade fairs. There were major fairs at Champagne and Lyons in France, Frankfurt in Germany and several cities in **Flanders**, including Bruges. Merchants who went to these fairs were quick to spot new fashion trends. On their travels afterwards, they spread these fashions far and wide.

MATERIAL MATTERS

Three areas of Europe became important textile-making centres at this time. Weavers in Northern Italy made silk **damasks** and velvets, as well as **cloth of gold**. The silk cloth above came from the famous Italian silk-weaving city of Lucca. People from Ghent and other parts of Flanders made top-quality fabrics using wool from England. The Spanish made excellent silks (see page 27). They were also expert leatherworkers and produced fine leather shoes. The most valuable leather goods were dyed red with **kermes**.

EUROPE IN THE FOURTEENTH CENTURY

During the early fourteenth century, costume in Europe changed little. But as the era of learning and discovery later known as the **Renaissance** began in Italy, a new interest in the human form began to inspire fashion, too. From the middle of the century, men's and women's clothing styles changed dramatically right across the continent.

This Italian woman is wearing a decorated silk overgown on top of a plain undergown. Overgowns of this type were also popular in northern Europe, where they were often known as cotehardies.

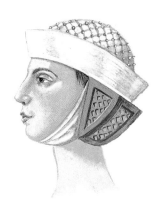

Medieval women often covered their hair in caps known as **cauls**. In this Danish caul, a jewelled hair net is enclosed in a linen and metal casing.

Shorter styles

Gradually men's long tunics and **surcoats** were replaced by short tunics known as **doublets**. They ended well above the knee, sometimes even on the hips, and were worn with shaped, close-fitting **hose**. The hose legs, which in the past had been separate, were joined to form a single garment. They were usually laced to the doublet to stop them from falling down.

A tight fit

The loose **super-tunic** worn by women was replaced by a more tight-fitting gown sometimes called a **cote**. It was **tailored** to fit the upper part of the body, but often flared out from the hips. A belt was often worn round the hips to emphasize their shape. Many women in England and **Flanders** wore the new sideless surcoat (see page 5) on top of their gowns. This garment was cut away above the hips so that the cote and belt could be seen underneath.

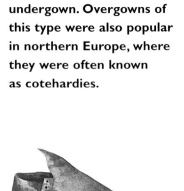

Shoes with long, pointed toes became popular at the end of the fourteenth century. They originally came from Poland and were called poulaines.

Houppelandes

In about 1360 a new garment called the houppelande was introduced for both men and women. This was a full gown and could be ankle-length or calf-length. It had a high neck, flared sleeves and sometimes a belted waist. Its edges were often cut into points, leaves or other shapes called dagges. Many garments were decorated in this way.

Royal courts often employed a jester to entertain people. Jesters wore short tunics and pointed hats with bells. They also carried a pig's bladder, as a sign of their profession.

MATERIAL MATTERS

The Moors, a Muslim people from North Africa, ruled much of Spain for several centuries during the Middle Ages. There they established a silk-making industry, and fine Moorish silks were still made after the Christians reconquered Spain. The fabrics were very highly prized and from time to time Spanish rulers tried to limit their use. For example, the fourteenth-century Spanish king Alfonso XI issued a sumptuary law (see page 29) stating that only he and his sons could wear silk when they chose. The rich could wear gold embroidered silks once only – for their weddings.

Dress Discovery

In 1921, archaeologists discovered many examples of medieval dress in an old churchyard at Herjolfsnes, Greenland, where Norwegian settlers had once lived. Some of the garments still had skeletons inside. The clothes were made of wool and showed that the fashions of mainland Europe had reached the island. They included a woman's gown, a man's coat and many hats and hoods (above left). The discovery gave costume experts useful information about clothing in the **Middle Ages**.

SHORT AND LONG FOURTEENTH CENTURY

The Englishman on the left is dressed very fashionably. His short doublet is made of woven silk and he wears a jewelled belt round his hips. Streamers, called **tippets**, hang down from the elbows. On top of the doublet, the man wears a short cape with a hood attached at the back. He is not wearing any shoes because his hose are a special kind that have soles attached.

The man on the right is wearing a dagged, calf-length houppelande. It is belted at the waist and has wide, flared sleeves. On his head he wears a hood with a dagged collar attached. On top of that another hood is worn as a hat, with the top pulled over his forehead.

EUROPE IN THE FIFTEENTH CENTURY

A gondolier from Venice, Italy. The picture shows the type of brightly patterned garments often worn by young men in that city.

Babies in a carrying basket – the handle at the top was balanced on the shoulder. Medieval babies were wrapped in linen strips known as swaddling clothes.

During the fifteenth century, European costume became more luxurious. The people of Italy, Spain and **Burgundy** wore the most splendid clothes of the period, but everywhere the rich wore garments that shouted 'look at me'.

Shorter and shorter

Men's **doublets** became even shorter in this era. They were usually close-fitting with tight waists and padded chests and hips. As the **hose** tops could now be seen, the join between the legs was often covered with a fabric **codpiece**. Over their doublets, young men often wore a short, sleeveless robe that hung loose from shoulders to hem. Older men continued to wear the houppelande (see page 26) or a shorter version called the haincelin.

Glorious gowns

Early in the century, women wore the houppelande, but other gown styles became more popular. One fashion was to wear a loose robe over a close-fitting garment similar to a **cote**. The robe was belted under the breasts, then dropped to the ground in folds. It often had a V neck filled with a triangle of fabric. Women also began to shape their bodies with stiffened **bodices**.

Turning heads

People wore many different styles of hats and headresses during this period. Women's hats were often made from padded rolls of fabric that were formed into shapes such as horns or hearts. These perched on top of jewelled **cauls** (see right). The hennin (see box, right) was also popular. Both men and women wore various kinds of hoods. Men also liked **chaperons** with long **liripipes** attached (see right).

This man is dressed in a style of coat that was fashionable in Italy. The rich fabric is tied at the waist with a thick cord that has a purse attached.

The man above wears a chaperon. It has a padded section around his head, a short flap of fabric down one side and a long liripipe hanging on the other. The woman wears a padded heart-shaped roll with a caul covering her hair.

FRENCH ELEGANCE FIFTEENTH CENTURY

The Frenchman on the left wears a short red tunic with padded sleeves over a black doublet. His black hose end in long, narrow points – during this era the longest points measured more than half a metre. The black, cone-shaped hat on his head is decorated with a gold chain and brooch. A gold cross on a double neck-chain completes his outfit.

The woman on the right wears a belted, V-necked dress. It is made of crimson **cloth of gold** velvet and has a fur-trimmed collar, hem and cuffs. She wears a steeple-shaped headdress called a hennin, draped with a veil. The woman's hair cannot be seen. Experts think that women of the time may have plucked their foreheads.

Sumptuary Laws

In the **Middle Ages**, rulers often passed sumptuary laws that tried to limit who could wear fine fabrics and fancy clothes. They made these laws for many different reasons. The laws were, for example, a way of raising money, as people could be charged for wearing luxury items such as silk or furs. For the Church, the laws were a way of stopping people from dressing extravagantly, which was seen as sinful.

MATERIAL MATTERS

By the fifteenth century, medieval dyers in Europe had learned how to dye cloth deep, strong colours. Dark shades of blue, green and violet as well as black became very fashionable. Philip the Good, Duke of Burgundy (left), only wore deep blue, violet or black because the gems and gold of his jewellery showed up more clearly against dark colours.

MEDIEVAL CHINA

During the medieval period China was ruled by four Chinese **dynasties** and the **Mongol** Yuan. The main items of clothing had changed little since ancient times. But as one dynasty followed another, differences gradually developed.

Women's wear

Rich women dressed in long silk robes called *p'ao*. These usually wrapped over at the front and were fastened with sashes, belts or hooks. They were often worn with loose trousers and **stoles**. Small models found in tombs of the Tang dynasty show that robe styles changed regularly. Poor women usually wore trousers and short wrapover jackets made of **hemp**, cotton or wool. Sometimes they also wore long dresses.

Chinese women's 'lily feet' could fit into shoes that were 14 centimetres long.

These small statues of noblewomen are from the Tang dynasty. One wears a stylish, wide-sleeved robe and the other wears a simpler dress and hat suitable for riding.

Followers of fashion

Women often wore make-up. They coloured their lips red, powdered their faces with pollen and painted flowers on their cheeks. Hair was held in place with jewelled combs or bone pins. In the Song dynasty it became fashionable for females to have tiny 'lily feet'. Girls' feet were bound with cloth from the age of about five so that they could not grow properly. This was very painful.

Men's wear

Rich Chinese men and emperors dressed in long, full-sleeved *p'ao* robes made of silk. Some robes crossed over at the front, others fastened on one side. A Tang dynasty wall painting shows that emblems such as dragons were embroidered on royal robes. By the Ming dynasty there were 12 symbols on emperors' garments, including fire and pheasants. Poor men wore trousers and short, belted tunics made of fabrics such as hemp.

This short robe is made of yellow silk. It once belonged to Zhu Tan, a prince of the Ming dynasty.

Ordinary Chinese people dressed in a variety of simple, loose robes, jackets and trousers. Men and women often also wore hats made of cloth.

MATERIAL MATTERS

Far back in ancient times, the Chinese were the first people to discover how to make silk. By the Tang dynasty, silks were so popular that there were sumptuary laws (see page 29) to limit their use. The Chinese invented several new types of silk in the medieval period. They included silk tapestry, known as *kesi*. Many *kesi* designs showed characters from Buddhist stories. The fabric was used for wall hangings, screens and fans as well as for robes.

Modes of the Mongols

The Mongol Yuan dynasty ruled China from 1279 to 1368. Yuan emperors such as Khubilai Khan were fierce warrior horsemen. They spent much of their lives dressed in leather armour and iron helmets. They also carried bows and arrows, as well as wicker shields with a hard **lacquer** coating. Yuan emperors' wives, such as Khubilai's wife Chabi (left), wore silk robes, gold jewellery and big headdresses. They painted their faces white and their eyebrows black.

A LADY AND AN EMPEROR EIGHTH AND TENTH CENTURY

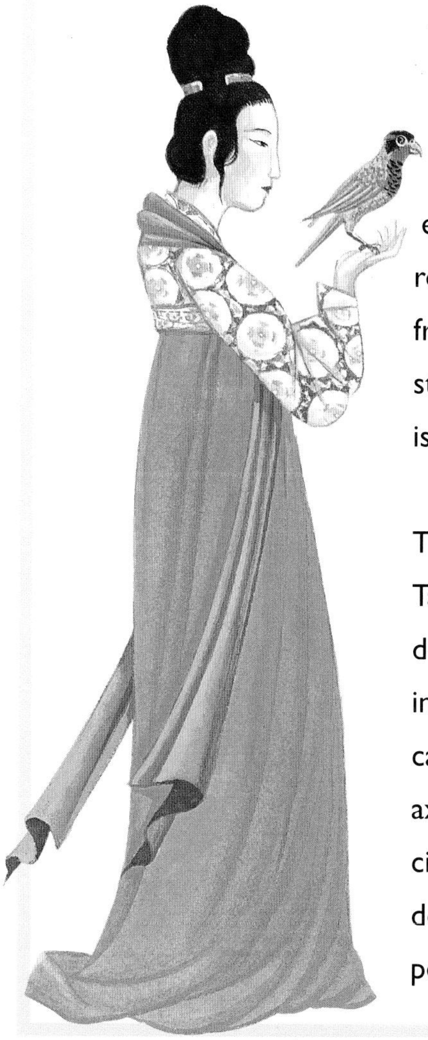

This picture of a lady is based on a painting found in an eighth-century Chinese tomb. She wears a long-sleeved robe that fits her upper body tightly, then falls in folds from a band below the breasts. She also has a red stole draped around her shoulders. The lady's hair is in a bun held in place with a bone clasp.

The magnificent figure on the right is Emperor Taizu. He is wearing a side-fastening robe decorated with imperial symbols. These include dragons and battle axes – you can see the blue and white blades of the axes near the bottom. A jewelled belt circles the emperor's waist and he has a decorated silk cap on his head. Satin boots peep out from under his robe.

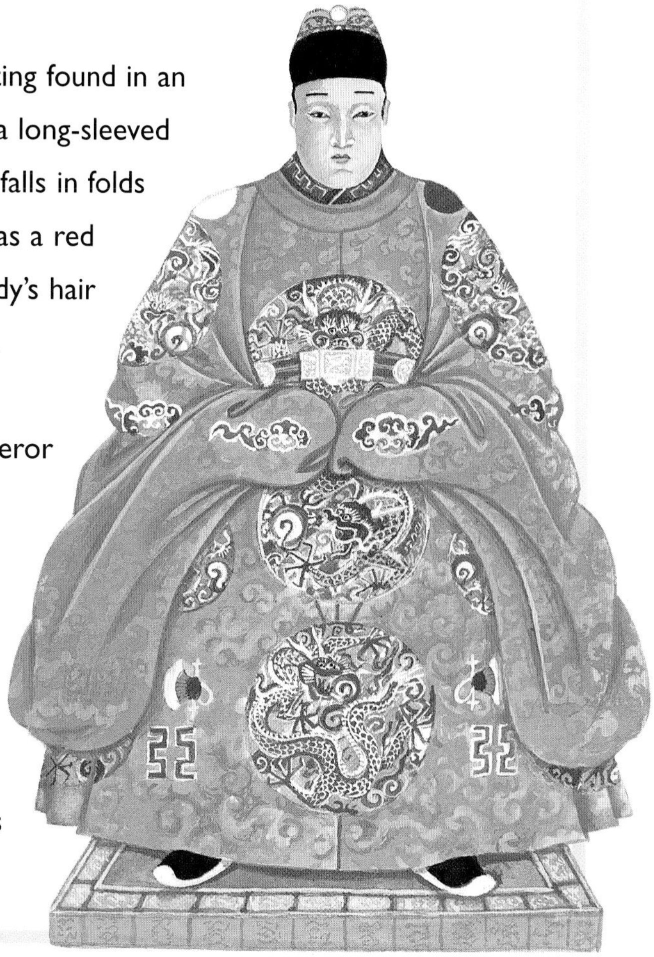

MEDIEVAL JAPAN

The most important item of clothing in medieval Japan was the kimono. The word simply means 'thing to wear'. Kimonos were based on Chinese *p'ao* robes. As time passed, they developed more and more special Japanese features.

Prince Shotoku Taishi ruled Japan from 593 to 622. Here he wears an early type of kimono that fastens at the side.

Kimono culture

Both men and women wore kimonos. These robes were long and full with wide sleeves. They could be worn belted or unbelted. At first kimonos often closed at the side. Later, a front-closing, dressing gown style was more common. Rich women sometimes wore up to 20 kimonos in contrasting colours at the same time. Loose trousers were worn under kimonos, and women especially liked to drape short **brocade** cloaks on the top.

Court costume

In the Nara Period the Japanese imperial family wore Chinese court robes. Later, by the Heian Period, the emperor's and empress's costumes were much more Japanese in style (see box, right). With his robes, the emperor wore ox-leather slippers covered in brocade. He also wore a silk *kanmuri* cap with a streamer on top. The empress wore a gold ornament in her hair that was shaped like a chrysanthemum flower.

The medieval Japanese often wore a simple type of sandal with raised wooden soles and straps made of cord.

Japanese women covered their skin with thick white powder. They also put black paint on their teeth so that they did not look dirty against the white.

Rich and poor

The garments of rich Japanese people were usually made of plain or patterned silks. Some silks were so fine that they were transparent. The clothes of the poor – kimonos or short, belted tunics worn with either trousers or skirts – were woven from rough plant fibres such as **hemp** and **ramie**.

The Japanese probably invented the folding fan, in about 670. Army generals carried fans as a sign of their status. The fans had sun symbols on one side, as shown, and moons on the other.

AN IMPERIAL COUPLE NINTH CENTURY

The emperor on the right is wearing his *sokutai* court robes. They have six separate layers – an inner pair of trousers (*okuchino*), an outer pair of trousers (*uwabakama*) and four robes, including one under-robe with a 4-metre train and a loose, outer *ho* robe. The *ho* is pulled up slightly over a jewelled belt. The emperor carries a wooden tablet called a *shaku*.

The empress on the left is dressed in her *junihitoe*, which means '12 layers'. Over various silk undergarments and kimonos she wears a short brocade jacket called a *karaginu*. This has a *mo* (train) of pleated white silk attached at the back. The full red outer skirt is known as a *nagabakama*. It is divided at the front.

Samurai Style

In the late twelfth century, military government was established in Japan. At this time, warriors called samurai began to play an important role in Japanese life. Samurai body armour was made of leather strengthened with iron plates covered in **lacquer** and joined with silk cords. The helmet often had a fierce face mask attached. Some helmets had horn-shaped crests. Samurai weapons included steel swords, skewers, bows and arrows.

MATERIAL MATTERS

Japan had no linen, cotton or wool. Poor people wore clothes made of plant fibres such as hemp, and the rich wore clothes made of silk. The Japanese wove fine, patterned silks, and also used dyeing techniques to make patterns on fabrics. Among them was *kanoko-zome*, a kind of tie-dyeing. Tradition tells how it was developed when an emperor asked some dyers to create cloths with spotted patterns. He wanted them to look like the dappled hides of deer fawns (*kanoko*) in his park.

MEDIEVAL AFRICA

In medieval times, Islam spread to North Africa (see pages 22–23), bringing great changes there. At the same time, several new states developed in Africa south of the Sahara Desert. Many different costumes were worn in this vast area, and most were made either of woven cloth or animal skins and furs.

These princes from the medieval kingdom of Ghana are dressed in robes that were woven locally from imported silk. They also wear headdresses of beaten gold.

Weaving skills

There were expert weavers in several areas of medieval Africa. Among the most skilled were the Yoruba of Nigeria and the Akan of Ghana. They used local cotton to produce fabric, which they dyed bright colours. Some of the fabric was used locally, the rest was carried along trade routes to North Africa. Fabric was also woven from silk. It came from silkworm cocoons or from unravelled imported cloths made of silk.

West African wear

Many of the greatest states in Africa grew up in the west. In the kingdom of Ghana princes dressed in draped robes made of silks from Muslim North Africa. They also wore glittering headdresses and gold jewellery. Many people of later empires in the area adopted both the religion and the loose, flowing robes of Muslims from the north.

Across the continent

On the east coast, Arab traders in long cotton tunics mixed with Africans in brightly dyed, draped robes and wrap-around skirts. In southern Africa, a great civilization flourished in the area of modern Zimbabwe from about 1200. People made copper jewellery, and probably wore woven tunics and loincloths. In many areas warriors and hunters covered themselves in animal skins.

This crown was worn by the rulers of Axum, a kingdom once in north-east Africa. Axum was at its height in the early medieval period.

A necklace of coral beads (top) and a gold ankle bracelet from the West African kingdom of Benin (see right).

A wooden dance mask made by the Igbo people. In medieval times, the Igbo lived in West Africa. Their descendants can still be found there today.

MATERIAL MATTERS

African weavers made fabric dyes from many plants. They included the henna shrub, whose leaves made a red-brown dye, the camwood tree, whose wood made a red dye, and indigo plants that produced blue dyes. Cola nuts were also used to dye cloth yellow, and charcoal to dye it black.

Tuareg Style

The Tuareg were nomads who roamed the Sahara Desert on camels – some still do. Both men and women dressed in long, loose cotton robes, and the men also wore veils that showed only their eyes. Tuareg garments were often dyed blue using **indigo** (see left). Jewellery made of silver, which the Tuareg prized more than gold, was very popular.

A MAN AND A MASK
FOURTEENTH AND FIFTEENTH CENTURY

In medieval times, several kingdoms emerged in what is now Nigeria. Among them was Ife, which was at its greatest in the fourteenth century. Ife was home to the Yoruba people (see far left). The illustration on the left, based on a statue, shows the oni (ruler) of Ife in ceremonial costume. He is dressed in a loincloth with a slanting hem. It has fringed ties that hang down from the waist on one side. He also wears many necklaces and anklets, and an ornamental hat.

The bronze mask on the right was made in the nearby kingdom of Benin, which was at its most powerful in the fifteenth century. The mask was given to the ruler of a neighbouring state, who wore it for important ceremonies. The oba (ruler) of Benin also wore bronze or ivory masks on special occasions.

THE INCAS

This short, sleeveless tunic was once worn by an Inca man. It is made from a cotton and wool mixture.

The Incas emerged in the Andes mountains of Peru in about 1000. Later, they built an empire around the city of Cuzco. In the reign of Emperor Pachacutec it grew to cover a vast area, from modern Colombia to Chile. Incas were excellent weavers and gold-workers, and wore the clothes and jewellery that they made.

The Inca necklaces above are made of gold and shell (above centre) and gold and turquoise (left to right).

Wool and weaving

The Incas made many garments from cotton and the wool of local animals, such as llamas and **vicuñas**. Eventually, only the Inca ruler, the Sapa Inca, was allowed to wear fine vicuña garments. Cloth was highly prized, so some wool animals were owned by the state. Weavers were also strictly watched. Women who made cloth for the ruler's garments were locked away. They often used backstrap looms (see page 41) for their work.

The Incas made decorated slings for hurling stones at their enemies. These examples are embroidered with llama wool.

Feathers and fur

The Incas used two other special materials for clothing. They wove feathers of tropical birds such as macaws and quetzals into cloaks for nobles and the Sapa Inca. The fur of jaguars, caught for the Incas by other tribes in the Peruvian jungles, was made into ceremonial robes.

Simple garments

Inca clothing was simple but colourful. Men dressed in loincloths, hipcloths or short tunics. Women often wore long dresses with short cap sleeves. Cloaks or shawls were sometimes draped on top. Clothes were decorated with embroidery, feathers and even gold ornaments. Important members of Inca society had the most decorated outfits. Inca shoes and sandals were made of rope or of soft leather dyed black, white, yellow and red.

The Sapa Inca wore a distinctive headdress with a tasselled fringe.

COTTON CLOTHING FIFTEENTH CENTURY

The Inca woman on the left is wearing a long cotton dress with short sleeves. Her decorated waistband has been made using embroidery and appliqué. Appliqué is a technique that involves sewing shaped pieces of one fabric on to another. The woman's sandals have rope soles and leather tops.

The two children on the right are wearing short cotton tunics. Inca tunics were not **tailored** to fit the body like many modern clothes, but were simply sewn down the sides. The elaborate embroidery on their tunics shows that the children come from the family of a high-ranking Inca official.

River Gold

The Incas and earlier Peruvian peoples loved gold, which they called 'the sweat of the sun'. They collected nuggets and flakes of gold from mountain rivers as the clear water carried them downwards. Craftsmen then turned the gold into all sorts of objects, including ceremonial weapons, funeral masks (above), necklaces and earrings. They even used gold to make short boots for women.

MATERIAL MATTERS

The chinchilla (below) is a small rodent with pale grey fur. It has more hairs in each square centimetre of its coat than any other animal. The Incas used its skins to make cloaks, and its fur to make chinchilla wool. This was produced by shearing the animals like sheep, then spinning the fur. The wool was woven into a fine, very soft cloth.

37

THE AZTECS

In about 1200 the Aztecs moved into the Valley of Mexico, Central America. There they built up a mighty empire, with the city of Tenochtitlán as its capital. The Aztecs wore garments made of cotton or of maguey fibre (see right). The clothes of the wealthy were decorated, the clothes of the poor were usually plain.

The Aztecs sometimes wore lip ornaments. This gold example is in the shape of a bird's head and was attached to the bottom lip.

This headdress, more than 1m tall, was worn by Aztec emperors. It is made of gold beads and tropical bird feathers. The long green feathers came from quetzals (see below).

Simple styles

Aztec men often wore just loincloths, but for warmth, they sometimes put cloaks called *tilmatl* on top. The cloaks were fastened with a knot on the right shoulder or in the middle of the chest. Nobles' cloaks were brightly dyed or embroidered. Women wore straight, calf-length skirts with short-sleeved or sleeveless *huipil* tunics on top. Sometimes the *huipils* were full-length and worn alone.

Fine feathers

Rich Aztecs loved to wear cloaks and headdresses made from the brightly coloured feathers of tropical birds such as parrots, quetzals and humming birds. Families who made feather garments lived in their own quarter of Tenochtitlán, the Aztec capital, and their skill was passed from one generation to the next.

War wear

Warriors wore uniforms in battle. Ordinary soldiers wore suits of quilted cotton that had been soaked in salt water to make them hard. Their helmets were made of leather or wood. Top-ranking knights wore jaguar skins. They climbed right inside and put their heads inside the jaguars' heads, which acted as helmets. Aztecs were armed with clubs, knives and spear-throwers. They carried cane and cotton shields covered with feathers or leather.

A quetzal's beautiful tail feathers are twice the length of its body. They shine and change colour with the light and were used to make some Aztec garments.

Officers of the Aztec army. Each army unit wore armour of a different design so that officers could recognize their own troops easily.

MATERIAL MATTERS

Poor Aztecs wore garments of rough maguey cloth, which was made from the fibres of the maguey cactus (below). The fibres were sometimes coloured before weaving, using dyes made from plants, insects and snails. All Aztec weaving, of cotton or maguey, was done by women.

Heading North

Many cultures flourished in North America during medieval times. Among them were the Hohokam and Anasazi peoples of the south-west, who had trading links with Aztec Mexico. Both bought and wore Mexican items such as shell bracelets, parrots' feathers and turquoise gemstones. In the south-east, several groups lived in the Mississippi Basin area. Imprints of fabrics left by chance on pottery suggest that they wove and probably wore fabrics rather like **burlap** and **muslin**.

A MAN AND A WOMAN FIFTEENTH CENTURY

The man on the left is dressed in a loincloth tied in the Aztec style so that the ends hang loose at the back and the front. On top he wears a cloak fastened with a central knot. Both garments are highly decorated, showing that the wearer is rich. The man also has several pieces of gold jewellery – a chest ornament, two bracelets and two leg decorations.

The woman on the right is dressed in a two-piece cotton outfit of skirt and sleeveless *huipil* tunic. Both garments have fringed hems and are brightly embroidered. On her head, the woman wears a headband tied in a bow at the back and the front. On her feet she has sandals that are tied on around her ankles, but that are otherwise completely open.

MATERIAL MATTERS

Here you can find out more about some important medieval clothing materials.

King Richard II of England, who ruled from 1377 to 1399. His cape and cloak lining are made of ermine furs. The small black marks are the tips of the animals' tails.

Fur

Most furs used in medieval Europe came from Russia and were traded in the Russian city of Novgorod. Furs were often brought to the West by a northern European trading organization called the Hanseatic League. Rulers wore fur to show how important and rich they were. Clothes-makers used 20,000 **vair** furs in just 18 months to make clothes for the French king Charles VI. English kings often wore robes trimmed with **ermine**.

Leather

To make leather, the hair has to be removed from animal skins. Then the skins have to be **tanned** to prevent them from rotting. In the late **Middle Ages**, sumach leaves (see above) were often used for the tanning process. The finest leather of the medieval period was made in Cordova, Spain. Cordovan leather was naturally soft and white, but it was often dyed bright colours. Craftsmen sometimes also decorated it with patterns in gold and silver.

Wool

Wool was used to make clothes in many parts of medieval Europe, and much of it came from England. In about 1100, monks and landowners began to keep flocks of sheep and to sell wool abroad. Huge amounts went to **Flanders**, where it was turned into cloth. From the fourteenth century, the English also exported finished cloth. New techniques and machines helped the wool industry to become more successful. For example, spinning wheels replaced spindles (see right) and produced better yarn.

Some types of sumach leaves contain up to 30 per cent **tannin**. In medieval times they were powdered and used for tanning.

Wool has to be spun before it can be woven. An early method was to put the wool on a stick (above) and tease out one strand into a notch on a spindle (left). The spindle was turned to pull more of the wool into thread.

By the fourteenth century, wheels like this were used in Europe for spinning wool into thread. The wheel was turned by hand.

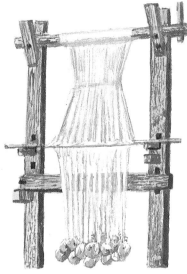

The Vikings used looms like this to make wool cloth. The weights at the bottom kept the vertical (warp) threads stretched tight. The horizontal (weft) threads were then woven through them.

Cotton

Cotton is spun from the bolls (seed pods) of cotton plants, then woven into fabric. It was widely used among the peoples of the Americas. For instance the Incas produced fine thread by turning the boll fibres around a spindle. Weaving was done on backstrap looms. One end of the backstrap loom was strapped around a weaver's back, and the other end tied to a post or tree. Cotton was also popular and valued in parts of Africa. In some places, such as Zaïre, only men were allowed to weave cotton cloth.

This illustration is based on a fourteenth-century picture. It shows two weavers operating a loom using foot pedals. They had to throw a shuttle carrying the woollen weft thread backwards and forwards between them. The boy at the front is preparing thread for the shuttle.

This beautiful piece of yellow silk was probably made in Sicily (see page 19) during the thirteenth century. Birds and dragons are woven into the cloth.

Linen

Linen is made from the stems of a plant called flax. In early medieval times linen was expensive, and was worn mainly by rich people. Linen is softer than wool, so nobles and kings liked to have linen underwear as well as robes. Linen slowly became cheaper and was even used for peasants' *braies*. Fine linens were made in England and, later, Flanders. Linen is difficult to dye, so was usually left uncoloured.

Silk

Silk is woven from the yarn made by silkworms when they spin their cocoons. At first only the Chinese knew how to do this, but craftworkers in the Middle East and then in the **Byzantine Empire** discovered the secret and began to make silk fabrics of their own. Sicily, Spain and Italy became silk-making centres, too. In the Islamic world, men were forbidden to wear silk next to their skin. This was because the Qur'an, the holy book of Islam, teaches that people will wear silk in Paradise, and religious leaders thought that they should wait until then.

MEDIEVAL ACCESSORIES

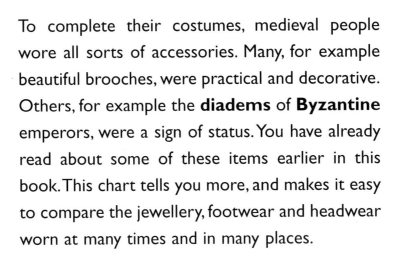

To complete their costumes, medieval people wore all sorts of accessories. Many, for example beautiful brooches, were practical and decorative. Others, for example the **diadems** of **Byzantine** emperors, were a sign of status. You have already read about some of these items earlier in this book. This chart tells you more, and makes it easy to compare the jewellery, footwear and headwear worn at many times and in many places.

	JEWELLERY	FOOTWEAR	HEADWEAR
BYZANTINE EMPIRE	Rich Byzantines wear plenty of heavy jewellery. Gold, bronze, rubies, emeralds and **enamel** are popular. Favourite items include crosses worn round the neck and crescent-shaped earrings.	Many types of shoe are made of dyed leather or cloth, and held on with laces or buttons. Emperors' shoes are often made of purple silk or red leather and decorated with pearls. Men also wear leather boots.	Byzantine men rarely wear hats. Some wear Phrygian caps with soft floppy points. Women often cover their long hair in nets decorated with pearls. Rulers wear jewelled diadems.
FRANKS	The Franks develop jewellery that includes Scandinavian, Roman and Eastern designs. They make brooches in many shapes, including birds of prey and serpents. Women love to wear enamel earrings.	Men wear leather shoes that are usually held on by laces tied round the foot or by strips of leather wound round the calves. Women's leather shoes are decorated with patterns. Some wear cloth shoes.	Early Frankish men go bareheaded, but later some wear soft hats made of cloth. Many have naturally red hair, others dye it red. Women, especially in the Carolingian era, cover their hair with jewelled nets.
ANGLO-SAXONS	The Anglo-Saxons make beautiful items of jewellery from pieces of enamel set in precious metals such as gold. Slivers of the red gemstone garnet are used in a similar way, for example to make belt buckles.	Both men and women wear simple leather shoes, which often have long, pointed toes. Some are slip-ons, others are held in place with leather thongs. Men especially wear leather boots fastened with laces.	Women cover their heads with veils called coverchiefs. Men often wear leather skullcaps or soft Phrygian caps. By late Anglo-Saxon times men often have long hair, but Christian priests disapprove.
VIKINGS	The Vikings are expert metalworkers who make brooches and pendants from gold, silver and bronze. They make necklaces by threading glass or amber beads on wires. Amber is used to make lucky charms.	Shoes are plain and made of cow leather or more expensive goatskin. Many are slip-ons, but others have buckles or straps that people adjust for fit. Men sometimes wear short or knee-length laced boots.	Men go bareheaded or wear simple cloth or leather skullcaps. In battle they put on protective iron helmets, which sometimes have neck and eye guards. Women normally wear a scarf knotted at the back and sides.
11TH- & 12TH-CENTURY EUROPE	Brooches are among the most popular jewellery items. Many are in the shape of a ring, but with a small gap breaking the circle. The finest are made of gold and gemstones. Enamel crosses are worn.	Both men and women wear leather shoes with pointed toes. They are often held on with a narrow, buckled or buttoned strap round the ankle. Sometimes the toes are shaped to look like scorpion tails.	Women cover their hair with veils. These are often held in place with circlets of **braid** round the head. Men often go bareheaded, but sometimes pull up hoods attached to their gowns or capes.

JEWELLERY	FOOTWEAR	HEADWEAR	
Islamic teaching does not allow the use of precious materials such as gold or gems. Some were still made into jewellery in medieval times, but most were later melted down so the metal could be reused.	Across the Middle East and Islamic North Africa, people usually wear open sandals or slipper-style shoes made of leather or cloth. Outside, women often wear outdoor slippers over their indoor slippers.	Arab men often wear turbans. The cloth is sometimes wound round a brimless cap with a point. Women dress modestly. They often pull their cloaks over their hair and wear face veils.	ISLAMIC WORLD
Brooches are still used to fasten garments. Crosses are widely worn, as well as pendants that hold relics of saints. These may be bones, teeth or scraps of clothing worn by a saint. Most are fake.	Pointed leather shoes are still in fashion, but not scorpion tails. Peasants wear shoes made of wood or with wooden soles and cloth or leather uppers. They often wrap animal skins round their legs for warmth.	Women often wear veils with a wimple, a piece of fabric that covers the neck. Their hair is often tucked into a net with a fillet (circle of linen) on top. For men, linen caps called coifs are popular.	13TH-CENTURY EUROPE
Pearls and precious metals are used, not just for jewellery, but to ornament items of clothing, too. Belts and headdresses are decorated with gold and gems. Necklines are often edged with glittering jewels.	Shoes called poulaines come into fashion. Their long toes are kept in shape by stuffing and whalebone. People wear pattens (wooden overshoes) to protect them from the muddy streets.	Jewelled hair nets called cauls become popular for women. They are often worn as part of complicated headdresses that include stiff linen fillets or padded rolls. Men often wear draped hoods.	14TH-CENTURY EUROPE
Jewelled clothing styles become more extravagant. Gold necklaces and collars are worn by men and women. On special occasions rich women sometimes drape gold or coral necklaces round their gowns.	Pointed shoes are worn until about 1490, when they are replaced by square-toed shoes. Some men wear boots over light shoes. Others wear **hose** that have soles attached (first worn in the 14th century).	Women wear ornate headdresses, including steeple-shaped hennins with veils draped on top. Padded rolls shaped like hearts and horns are worn with cauls. Many men wear **chaperons**.	15TH-CENTURY EUROPE
Jewellery is usually made of silver and often covered in blue enamel. Jade is the most popular stone. Belts are made of jewels and precious metal. Officials wear jewelled buttons on their hats to show their rank.	From about the 10th century young girls have their feet bound, so that they remain tiny. They wear cloth shoes, but walking is painful. Men also wear cloth shoes – emperors' were often satin.	Men often wear hats of folded cloth. Rich women hold hairstyles in place with jewelled combs or bone pins. Empresses wear headdresses of blue-enamelled silver and gold. These often feature bird designs.	MEDIEVAL CHINA
Jewellery is made of gold, ivory and lacquer. Jewelled buttons are popular. The *netsuke* (carved toggle) is used to fasten waist sashes around kimonos. It is made of ivory, bone, amber or other material.	Shoe styles include a sandal like a modern flip-flop with a raised sole. They are worn with special socks that separate the big toe from the others. Slipper-style shoes of cloth or leather are also popular.	Rich women sweep their hair into high, wide styles that they rub with oil and decorate with ornaments. Men wear hats of folded cloth. Emperors have silk *kanmuri* caps with streamers.	MEDIEVAL JAPAN
In West Africa gold is used for bracelets, anklets and other items. The Songhai make amber jewellery, while in Benin brass and ivory are popular. The Tuareg are famous for their silver jewellery.	South of the Sahara Desert people go barefoot or wear open leather sandals. In the Islamic North, slipper-style shoes of cloth or soft leather are popular, and men and women sometimes wear high boots.	The princes of Ghana wear headdresses of beaten gold, while the kings of Axum wear jewelled crowns. Women often wear brightly dyed headcloths. Tuareg men wear dark veils. Masks are worn for ceremonies.	MEDIEVAL AFRICA
The Incas make necklaces, earrings and other jewellery from gold, which they call 'the sweat of the sun'. Shell and turquoise are used too. Aztecs loved to wear gold chest ornaments, bracelets and leg clasps.	Both Incas and Aztecs go barefoot or wear open sandals that have rope soles and leather uppers. The leather is often dyed black, white, yellow or red. The Aztecs sometimes decorate sandals with feathers.	Inca men often wear brightly coloured wool caps. The Inca ruler had a distinctive headdress with a tasselled fringe. Aztecs and Incas wore feathered headdresses for special occasions.	AZTECS & INCAS

MAPS OF THE MEDIEVAL WORLD

Many of the empires, countries, regions and cities of the medieval world were known by names that we no longer use. The maps on these pages will help you to locate where they were. The world map shows the area that each of the three detailed maps covers.

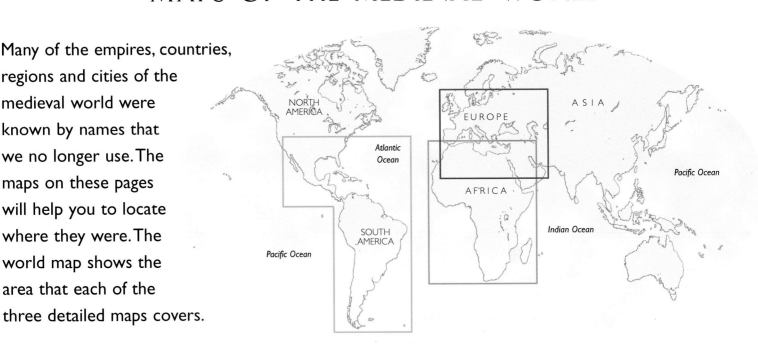

Inca c.1000–1533
Aztecs c.1200–1521
Anasazi c.700–1500
Hohokam c.400–1450

1

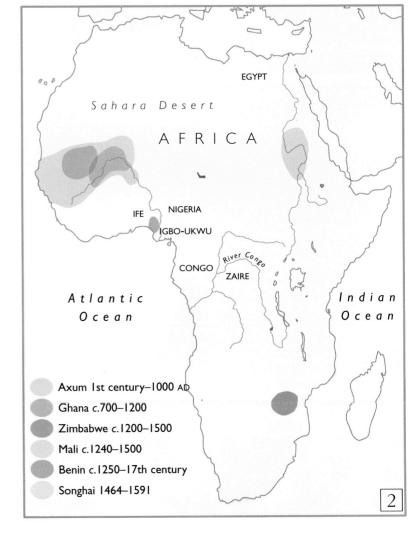

Axum 1st century–1000 AD
Ghana c.700–1200
Zimbabwe c.1200–1500
Mali c.1240–1500
Benin c.1250–17th century
Songhai 1464–1591

2

The three detailed maps on these pages show:
1. South America and part of North America
2. Africa
3. Europe, the Middle East, North Africa and Western Asia.

They include places that existed at different times during the period covered by this book. Some modern country names have been included, to help you find your way around.

The main pages of the book, and the time strips that run along the tops of the pages, will tell you exactly when each place played a major part in world history.

General key to place names
EUROPE   Continent name
DENMARK   Country name
FLANDERS   Region or empire name
Florence   City name

● Frankish Kingdom

● Byzantine Empire

3

GLOSSARY

alb A long white robe with narrow sleeves worn by Christian priests.

bodice A tight-fitting garment worn on a woman's upper body. It may be sleeved or sleeveless and is often fastened with laces.

braid Several strands of material plaited together.

braies A type of breeches with a drawstring waist worn by European men in the early Middle Ages.

breeches A trouser-like garment worn by men. In late medieval Europe there were many different styles, most finishing at the knee.

brocade A rich fabric with a raised pattern. The pattern was usually created using gold or silver threads.

Burgundy A region of eastern France that was an independent state during medieval times.

burlap A rough, plain material often woven from hemp.

Byzantine Empire The area ruled from the city of Constantinople (Greek name Byzantium) after the fall of Rome. The empire ended in 1453, when the city fell to the Ottoman Turks.

caftan A long, sleeved garment with a front opening that was originally worn in Persia and Central Asia. It was later adopted by Arabs, Turks, Byzantines and others.

caul A type of head covering worn by women in medieval Europe. There were many styles, but they all included a decorated hair net.

cavalry The part of an army whose members ride horses into battle.

chain mail A type of armour made from linked metal rings.

chaperon A style of hat for men. It had a stiff brim, a soft top and pieces of cloth hanging down each side.

chasuble A type of short cloak worn by Christian priests. It had a hole for the head but no sleeves.

chemise An undergarment shaped like a loose, long tunic.

cloth of gold A type of silk cloth with gold threads in the weave.

coat of arms A colourful design that a knight wore on his shield and helmet to represent his family.

codpiece A fabric bag joining the legs of men's hose at the front, below the waist.

cote A woman's gown that was close-fitting at the top but often flared at the hips.

Crusaders Soldiers who fought in the **Crusades** – a series of wars between Christians and Muslims in the Middle East between 1095 and 1270.

dalmatica A type of full-length tunic with long, wide sleeves once worn in Ancient Rome.

damask A type of woven cloth with a pattern that is clear on both sides.

diadem A large, open circle of gold or other precious metal worn as a type of crown.

doublet A tight-fitting, sleeved top worn by European men. Doublet styles changed over time in both length and shape.

dynasty A family that rules a country for generations.

enamel A glasslike substance that is made in many colours. Pieces of enamel are often set into metal to make items of jewellery.

ermine The special name for a small animal called a stoat when it lives in northern regions such as Russia. It is also the name of the stoat's white winter fur, which was often made into garments for kings and queens.

feudal organized according to the feudal system.

feudal system A social system that spread across much of Western Europe from the eighth century. Kings, who owned all the land, were at the top of the system. They loaned land to nobles, who loaned it to knights. Knights loaned it to peasants. In return for the land, people had to provide services, such as fighting for the king in war.

fibula (plural **fibulae**) A type of brooch used to fasten garments.

Flanders A medieval state that included areas now in Belgium, the Netherlands and northern France. It was famous for its fine wool cloth.

fresco A type of painting made by applying paints to wet plaster.

Germanic Of or relating to people who originally came from the regions of modern Scandinavia and Germany.

helm A simple, early type of helmet worn by European knights. Helms had no visors, so wearers had to peer through eye slits.

hemp A type of plant grown in Asia. Poor people often used its tough fibres to make a kind of coarse cloth.

hose A type of leg covering for men. Until the tenth century, hose covered the lower leg, like socks. Later they became longer and were attached to the bottom of the tunic with laces. In the fourteenth century, hose legs were joined at the top, rather like modern tights.

indigo A deep blue dye made from the indigo plant, which lives in parts of Africa and other tropical regions.

kermes A red dye made from the crushed bodies of insects that belong to an insect group named *Kermes*. Only female insects could be used to make the dye.

lacquer A type of hard, shiny coating made of tree resin.

liripipe A thin piece of material up to about 2m long that was attached to a chaperon hat. It often hung loose at the side, but could also be draped around the hat or body. It developed from a type of hood.

maniple A strip of material that a Christian priest draped over his left arm. It was originally a type of napkin.

mantle A type of long, loose cloak, often fastened with a cord linking two clasps at the neck.

Middle Ages The period of history that lasted from about 500 AD, after the collapse of the Roman Empire, to about 1500, shortly after the arrival of Europeans in the Americas.

Mongol A member of a people from Mongolia that rose to power under Genghis Khan in the early thirteenth century. The Mongol Yuan dynasty ruled China from 1279 to 1368.

muslin A type of plain, fine cotton fabric. The name comes from the city of Mosul in the Middle East, where it was first made.

Normans The name for the people of north-west France who were descended from the Vikings and who conquered England in 1066.

Orthodox Christianity The form of Christianity practised in the Byzantine Empire and later in Greece, Russia and other parts of eastern Europe. The Orthodox Church split from the Roman Catholic Church, based in Rome, in 1054.

p'ao robe A style of long, loose robe worn by Chinese men and women from ancient times.

ramie A fabric made from the stems of a nettle plant also called ramie.

Renaissance The era of European history in which people rediscovered the learning of the ancient world while making new advances in science, art and other areas. It lasted from about 1350 to 1550.

sable A weasel-like animal from northern Asia with a shiny, dark black or brown coat. Sable skins were often used to make fur garments.

Silk Road One of the ancient trade routes along which silk and other goods were carried from China to the West.

smelt To heat a rock containing a metal such as iron so that the metal comes out.

spurs Metal points that knights strapped to their feet and dug into horses' sides to make them go faster.

stole A strip of fabric like a shawl.

super-tunic A tunic worn on top of other garments. It was usually looser than the tunics underneath.

surcoat A usually sleeveless over-garment, often with low-cut sides.

tailor To cut, shape and sew cloth in order to make garments that fit the body well.

tan To treat animal hides with substances containing the chemical tannin. This process turns them into leather and stops them from rotting.

tannin A substance found in some plants and used to tan leather.

tippet A long, thin strip of cloth or fur attached to the elbow of a doublet or gown for decoration.

vair The name given to a type of fur used to decorate rich people's garments in the Middle Ages. Experts believe it may have come from a type of squirrel found in Russia.

vicuña A type of South American animal similar to the llama. The Incas used vicuña wool to make garments.

visor A hinged metal flap on the front of a helmet that can be raised so that the wearer can see clearly or lowered for protection.

Western Christian Empire A European empire that lasted from about 800 to 1806. The Frankish king Charlemagne was its first emperor. From 1254, the name Holy Roman Empire was often used for the peoples and lands in the same area.

INDEX